I0716123

The Laughing String

Thoughts on Writing

Stephen Evans

For those who wait for inspiration.

Third Edition

The Laughing String: Stephen Evans
ISBN: 978-1953725639
Time Being Media LLC

"And like a laughing string
Whereon mad fingers play
Amid a place of stone"

William Butler Yeats

STEPHEN EVANS

CONTENTS

FOREWORD

The ancient Greeks worshipped three entities linked to the idea of destiny:

Ananke, goddess of Necessity whose mate was Khronos, Time. The Moirai or the Fates, the three sisters who spun out the threads of life. And Tyche, the goddess of Fortune, who brought abundance.

In 1973, as a college freshman at Georgetown university, I auditioned for the musical *Man of La Mancha* at Mask & Bauble, Georgetown's student theater company. I had done some shows in high school and I liked to sing, but theater was a pastime for me. I attended Georgetown because I planned to go to law school after college.

The director said the callback list would be posted the next day outside the office of the theater, which at that time was in Poulton Hall just beyond the campus walls. So the next day, I walked all over Poulton Hall (which wasn't that large actually) looking for the callback list. I attended many classes that day, none of which were mine, in my quest. But I found no list.

Normally, I would have followed my introvert instincts and let it go. But this one time at least, I didn't. I went to the callbacks and walked up to the director, apologized, and said I couldn't find the list and I was wondering if I was called back for the show. He checked the list, looked at me, and said: "You know I wanted you in the show but forgot to put your name on the list".

So I ended up in that show, and several more, and spent more time at the theater than in any classroom. In my life, theater has been sometimes an occupation, often a preoccupation, and always an education.

I wonder sometimes at the chance that changed my life so (sorry, I can't help myself) dramatically. I wonder how in all my wandering that day I never took the few steps down to the theater office in the basement of Poulton Hall. I wonder if it was really an accident that my name was not on the list, or if the director was just being nice to the clearly confused freshman.

Never has one typo led to so much typing.

I don't know which entity controlled my steps that day: Necessity, Fate, or Fortune. But I think it was Fortune, because I have been given such abundance. Not material abundance (certainly), or personal abundance (though I have had a measure of that), or even creative abundance (work for me is mostly slow and arduous).

But of joy in creation?

True abundance.

Blooming Out of Season

There is one bloom on my azalea bush. The bush itself is nearly five feet tall and about that wide. It normally blooms in late May, a bit later than most in the area, and is spectacular then—a tide of pink-orange. But for some reason, one blossom has waited until now, end of summer, in stifling heat and humid weather, to appear. I don't know why.

My first play *The Ghost Writer* was produced in 1991. Then nothing produced or published for seventeen years, until my novel *The Marriage of True Minds* in 2008. It's not that nothing was happening during those years. I got married and divorced. I moved to Minnesota and back to Maryland. I gained friends and lost family. But nothing of mine appeared on stage or in print.

As of this writing, I think I am up to seventeen books, plus various screenplays floating round, and bunches of poems. Maybe now I'm blooming out of season too. And maybe that's not so bad.

All of the things that happened to me shape the work I am doing now. Even this little piece, for what it is worth, I could not have written in 1991. I don't think I would have noticed the bloom, or thought about it, or written about it.

I know one thing: that one azalea blossom is getting a lot of attention from the bees and butterflies.

WHY MY NOVEL IS SET IN MINNEAPOLIS

Some years ago, I lived in Minneapolis for a while. During that time, I came to love the town and the quaint Midwestern customs of its citizens.

For example, people smiled at you on the street—without asking for money. If you were lost, they gave you directions—without asking for money. They even assisted the elderly across the street. In DC, we use them as decoys for oncoming traffic.

Minneapolis was especially inspiring for me as a writer.

You could write about the Human Drama of Snow. Or use Snow as a Metaphor for the Universal Condition. Or hurt your back shoveling Snow so that you had more Time to Write. As Shakespeare wrote:

Snow is the Winter of our Discontent.

But during my residence there, the aspect of Minneapolis that I loved most was the chain of lakes inside the city limits. The prevailing theory is that a glacier created the lakes, though this story is less than credible to me since never once during my stay did a mile-high wall of ice come down from Canada.

Two separate paths circumnavigate the lakes of Minneapolis. The Outer Path is for Speeders: bikers, inline skaters, and other mobility enthusiasts. While I admired their balance, dexterity, and tight clothing, I always thought it was odd to be in such a hurry when you are traveling in a circle.

The Inner Path around the lakes is for Footers: joggers, walkers, and plodders like me. The Inner Path often floods during the spring thaw, forcing both Speeders and Footers onto the same ground. This is a recipe for disaster. There's just no getting around me.

I lived in the top two floors of a Victorian house only two blocks from my favorite of the lakes: Lake of the Isles, known for its urban wildlife. In the winter, around the south side of Lake of the Isles, you could sometimes sight the rare Snow Serpent, a Norse American cousin of the Loch Ness Monster, who hibernates in summer and prowls the icy lake in winter. Many a snowman has been devoured by this sly leviathan.

In the spring, an armada of Canadian geese invades the lake. Each evening, the royal navy embarks from the lakeshore to their island harbor, a squadron of goslings in regal tow.

Lake of the Isles is also known for, well, isles—two of them near the northwest lakeshore. The island closest to land is very close; I always felt that I could jump across the narrow channel, or in January, slide across. But I never did, because there was a small sign standing akilter near the shore and nearly covered by the tall grasses. The sign read 'Game Preserve', in wavering letters that might have been painted by webbed feet.

Of course, in my imagination, *Game Preserve* referred to some place magical and forbidden, to a Velveteen Rabbit Puff the Magic Dragon Chutes and Ladders sanctuary in a clearing hidden deep in the interior of the tiny island. How I wanted to ignore the sign and explore! But I never did.

After I left Minneapolis, the magical island continued to feed my imagination. I could never forget the lake, and the sign, and my urge to break the rules, step onto the island, and discover that forbidden sanctuary just beyond the tree line. So finally I created a character who could.

I wish there had been a bench, there where the path curves and the shore and the island almost touch. I think I might be there still.

MY UNBIASED OPINION

I have concluded that my novel entitled *The Marriage of True Minds* is the greatest short novel ever written.

To explicate my criteria and decision-making process regarding my novel entitled *The Marriage of True Minds*, let's examine some of the other fine contenders:

Heart of Darkness, Joseph Conrad: I never laughed once.

Breakfast at Tiffany's, Truman Capote: Does not appear to be set in Minneapolis.

The Death of Ivan Ilyich, Leo Tolstoy: The letters in this book look funny and I'm not entirely sure it was written in English.

A Portrait of the Artist as a Young Man, James Joyce: Has more than five words in the title.

To the Lighthouse, Virginia Woolf: Was not written by me.

So, to sum up, my novel entitled *The Marriage of True Minds* is the greatest short funny novel set in Minneapolis written by me in English with a title of not more than five words.

DILEMMA

Do you:

Write the story you want to write?

or

Write the story you want to read?

or

Write the story that wants to be written?

or

Is that a trilemma?

Stephen Evans

YOU MAY QUOTE ME

In the movie version of *Harvey*, the character of Elwood P. Dowd says, "Years ago my mother used to say to me... She'd say, 'In this world, Elwood, you must be'—she always called me Elwood—'in this world, Elwood, you must be oh so smart or oh so pleasant.' Well, for years I was smart. I recommend pleasant. You may quote me."

I do, obviously. It is one of my favorite lines in one of my favorite films. I don't see six-foot-tall rabbits (or none I'm admitting to). But sometimes I think that something like his transformation may have happened to me. For years, I was smart, but being smart didn't make me a writer.

Twenty years ago, I decided I was supposed to be a writer. I thought about writing. I read books about writing. But I wasn't actually doing any writing.

So, feeling the years slipping by, I quit my job and headed out across the country, intending to write a book. Yet mile after mile, I wrote nothing, except a few emails about the amazing scenery and how often I got lost. Eventually, I gave up and turned toward home.

A thousand miles or so later, a butterfly got caught in my windshield wipers. I slowed down and got off the highway at the next opportunity, coaxed the little guy onto a sheet of (blank, no doubt) paper, and set him onto a patch of grass near some woods. He couldn't fly anymore, but he could walk. I watched each slow, painstaking step until he disappeared into the brush. Then I got back in my car and on the highway.

Moments later, a poem came to me about the butterfly. Quickly, I dictated the words into my recorder. It wasn't great poetry. But it was the first creative writing I had done in a long time.

That night, I sat at a desk in my hotel room and began to write. I didn't stop until I had finished the entire first act of a play, and then, over the next few years, finally a book about that trip: *A Transcendental Journey*.

Since I wrote *A Transcendental Journey*, so much of my life has revolved around taking care of family—a time that has also been the most creative of my life. I think there is a connection.

I began *The Marriage of True Minds*, my first novel, while I was taking care of my aunt Margaret, to whom it is dedicated. I edited the novel while staying with my friend Don in what turned out to be the last months of his life. The final piece of the story was based on the eulogy I wrote for my brother Michael.

A few years later, when both of my parents were diagnosed with health issues, I moved in to take care of them. My writing during those years consisted mostly of short pieces. But I think it is some of my best work.

After my parents passed away, I was lucky to be able to take some time off. I thought I needed it—needed to get back to being the person I used to be.

I never did.

I don't think now I will.

And I wouldn't choose to if I could, as a man or as a writer.

In my year off, I wrote drafts of two books, plus half of a third. Two were published in 2018: *The Island of Always,* an extension of *The Marriage of True Minds,* and *Painting Sunsets:* a Story for Young Artists. The third book, *Funny Thing Is: A Guide to understanding Comedy,* was published the following year.

I don't really like the word *caregiving;* it is too one-sided. Caring for someone is a shared experience, often both deeply rewarding and deeply draining. But in each case in my life, I feel that some reflection of that shared experience, and of the person I shared it with, has gone into the work.

As a writer, my instinct is to wrap myself up in a solitary world—to live in the one I am creating. But I have realized that what works for me may be the opposite.

Turn out, see the world, do what needs to be done for the people in your life. And as you do, trust that the wheels are turning in your creative spirit.

Caring is the wildest fuel for the writing fire.

You may quote me.

WHERE I WRITE

What constitutes writing?

If it's only where you type the words into your computer, then my writing space is not particularly exciting. It consists of a tiny lime green desk that once inhabited my mother's sewing room. Hanging on the wall above is a picture of the Iowa farm where my father grew up.

But if you count as writing the imaginative time that comes before the typing and reading and editing, then my writing space gets more interesting, and beautiful.

Several years ago, after a difficult family time, I decided to take some time off from work to catch up on writing projects I had been thinking about for years but had not had the time or energy to tackle. It ended up being nearly a year, not because I intended to take that much time, but because it took months longer to find a new job than I planned.

During this sabbatical, I was able to write drafts of two books: *The Island of Always*, the sequel to a novel I had published a while before and *Painting Sunsets*, a middle-grade fantasy novel I have had in the back of my mind for more than two decades. I also wrote a one-act play about Ralph Waldo Emerson entitled *Monuments,* which we hope to produce this summer. And finally I drafted a good deal of content for a book on comedy. It was a very good year.

Before this period, my writing process had always been to sit down at the computer and see what happened. But this year, my process changed.

Behind my condo, there is a little park that residents of the community refer to as the Broadwalk. The park is narrow, maybe 100 yards wide and half a mile or so long, with apartments and townhouses lining either side.

Down the middle of the park, an asphalt path wanders with no particular sense of purpose, willing to get there when to gets there. Benches are spaced along the way, for those of us who like to sit and think. Or just sit and breathe.

On either side of the path, trees and bushes and flower beds measure your progress. In the early spring, forsythia, skinny stairways made of sunshine, and jonquils, upside down bells of yellow gold, ring in the change of season. In late April, azalea paint the path in pastels (including light purple, like this sentence). A few weeks later, the dogwoods bloom throughout the grounds, myriad pink and white lace handkerchiefs waving in the breeze.

But the mature trees are year-round joys. The community was developed 50 years ago, and many of the trees are that old or more. The variety is notable, from oaks to poplars to birches and many more. About half the path is shaded by these welcome neighbors.

Every day, or at least every nice day, before sitting down to write, I got in the habit of taking a walk, hoping the creative space in my head would mirror the calm and beautiful space outside. Around noon, or maybe 1:00 PM, I would head outside, turn left (always the same direction) and stroll for about 45 minutes down the path, past dogs and humans in equal numbers. Having no dog I was often the odd man out and about, nodding to the humans and saying hello to the dogs.

I never really had the sense that I was writing. But by the time I had made the turn for home, my mind had also turned to the next scene, and I was deep in my creative space. My pace would pick up, because I knew exactly what my approach would be, often my exact words, and wanted to get to the keyboard without delay.

Though once in a while, something halted the stream of thoughts and images, diverted it into a different track. Then the beginnings of a new poem or a story would begin take shape.

What more can you ask of an office than to offer you stories to tell?

GNOSTIC FICTION

My father was a wonderful storyteller, and one of his favorite phrases was:

"I just tell them. I don't explain them."

I think among storytellers there is a lot to be said for that policy. But I have a notion about stories that I have been thinking about for a long time. I like to call it Gnostic Fiction, though I think it applies not just to fiction but to all narrative modes.

Gnosticism is a set of philosophical and/or religious ideas of uncertain origin. *Gnosis* is an ancient Greek word that translates roughly to knowledge. In Gnosticism, the path to salvation is through knowledge of the ultimate truth.

As a comedy writer, I am especially attracted to Gnosticism because of its basic tenet that the world we know is the result of some primal cosmic screwup. Which sounds about right to me.

But for me, Gnosticism also suggests a blueprint for telling a story, one I have attempted to follow in various works, including my novel *The Marriage of True Minds*. The idea is this. In Gnostic thought, the world as generally experienced is this world of error. But an understanding of true reality is available to those who pursue it, who are able to recognize the keys, and who are open to and prepared for the greater vision.

I like the idea of applying this multi-track reality concept to storytelling. I know that many writers construct hierarchies of meaning within texts. But I like to use the most obvious textual track (I don't think in hierarchies, with their implicit values, but more in tracks or threads through the text) to tell a story primarily for its entertainment value. By separating the deep meaning of the text from the reader's initial experience of the story, you can lighten the load and create the possibility of a purely entertaining event, a good thing in my view.

For those readers who want more (or, as I have discovered, mostly for my own amusement), you can place keys within the text leading to one or more alternate tracks of meaning, kind of like those magic quest video games where you pick up objects of power along the journey. These keys seem almost but not quite natural within the story experience, not enough to disrupt the reader's flow through the entertainment track, but enough that in retrospect, the keys call out for further attention.

I'm sure there are many ways writers can create these alternate tracks within a text. I tend to use architecture (structure is meaning, I like to say, always in my most meaningful voice).

In my play, *The Ghost Writer*, I use a convergence of archetypes. In *A Transcendental Journey*, I worked with what I called textual pointillism. In *The Marriage of True Minds*, I used an evolving point of view that meets up with the plot in chapter Eight.

Whether any of this actually works is an open question (though I think it does). And there are probably those who would argue that writers should say what they have to say in the clearest way possible.

But I think there is value in letting the reader choose the experience they want each time through. Which makes each time through a different experience of story and meaning.

I find that thought appealing. When you don't have a lot of readers, you want them to read as often as possible.

STEPHEN EVANS

THE MATURE WRITER

Most writers will tell you that once you finish a draft of a book, you have to put it away for a while, so you can approach it fresh, see without preconception what you wrote rather what you think you wrote. When I was younger, I would sometimes put a work in my metaphorical drawer for a year or more before looking at it again.

But as a mature writer, I find that is no longer necessary. Thanks to my declining memory, by the time I turn on the computer the next morning, it's as if I had never seen the words before. The tricky part now is remembering I wrote it in the first place.

Then again...what were we talking about?

WRITER'S BLOCK

Writer's block sometimes stems from worrying whether what you write will be good enough.

I don't have that problem. I know that what I write won't be good enough. But I write it anyway, so I can make it good enough.

And you can.

Always.

THE ANGEL BEHIND THE WINDOW

There is a legend that, when Michelangelo was carving a sculpture of an angel for the Basilica of San Domenico, a small boy asked what he was doing. The artist replied that he saw an angel in the marble and carved till he set him free.

I say legend because I can't find a source for the quote. Though in a letter to fellow Florentine Bennedetto Varchi, Michelangelo explained that the sculptor works by removing what is superfluous. Not as poetic but a similar thought.

I am working on a new play now, and for me, the dynamic seems slightly different (not that that surprises me). I think of the work, the angel, hidden behind a window covered with ice. Some parts of the ice are thicker than others. In the beginning, nearly all is obscured. I don't have the vision of a Michelangelo. But I can still see through the blurry frame that something interesting might be there.

As I write, I chip away at the ice. Each draft, a little bit of the ice falls away and a bit more of the final work shows through.

Though sometimes, when I chip at the ice on one part, another part freezes over again. Other times, what I think is ice is just my breath fogging the cold window.

It can be very frustrating. And I never eliminate all the ice and get to see the work as it should be.

But I keep trying. I know the angel is there behind the window, waiting to be revealed.

THE NEXT STEP

Today by email I got two rejections.

The first was a rejection from an agent I had queried about a children's book. The second was a rejection of a poem by a literary magazine.

It is not unusual for me to get a rejection. Like most writers, the contrary is true. Blue moons are common compared to acceptance for me.

But two on one day is unusual. It made me take note of my reaction.

For both, I went looking for the next place to submit. Rejection no longer seems like a denial of who I am, or even a commentary on what I have done. It is just the next step in the process of getting the work in the right hands.

I thought today it is like finding a place to plant a flower (something even more uncommon for me than blue moons). You need to find the right spot.

This soil is too acidic.

This has too little sun.

STEPHEN EVANS

This doesn't get enough rain.
I want my flower to bloom.
It takes a while to find just the right spot.

WHAT WOULD SHAKESPEARE DO?

In a letter to his brothers, Keats expressed admiration for what he called Negative Capability:

"I had not a dispute but a disquisition with Dilke, on various subjects; several things dovetailed in my mind, & at once it struck me, what quality went to form a Man of Achievement especially in literature & which Shakespeare possessed so enormously—I mean Negative Capability, that is when man is capable of being in uncertainties, Mysteries, doubts without any irritable reaching after fact & reason."

(Thank you, Wikipedia).

The modern interpretation of Keats's idea seems to be that the poet (or playwright) negates his/her own persona to inhabit that of the character. This is probably a good thing for a playwright. Certainly one can wander forever through Shakespeare looking for him in his characters.

But I don't think that's what Keats was getting at. I think he meant that sometimes art is messy. You can't quite pin it down; it keeps shifting. And not in a postmodern way, in the act of interpretation (or lack thereof), but in an epistemological or even ontological way, in that you are trying to say something that can't yet be said. Or maybe it's the recognition that world is messy and can't be contained by ordered Aristotelean unities.

I have been thinking about negative capability recently, because I am considering writing a follow-on book to my novel *The Marriage of True Minds*. At the end of that book, my principal characters are facing one another at a lakeshore, one kneeling on the water proclaiming his love for the other.

Apparently some readers would like to know what happens to these characters. I know this because they have asked me, or complained to me. I think it's great that they care. And honestly, I'm fond of these characters. So I would to like to know myself what happens next. And the only way to know is to write it. Right?

But I also like thinking of them there, suspended forever at that lake, in that moment. That uncertainty, that Mystery, seems right. Seems true, to them, and to me.

But do I have the negative capability to leave them there?

What would Shakespeare do?

Author's Note: Apparently I am not negatively capable as I did write the sequel, and the next, and I'm working on the next.

JUST BETWEEN US

I was taking a walk yesterday and thinking about the sequel to the sequel of my current endeavor, when it occurred to me that something I wrote almost 40 years ago in college would fit nicely into that book, which I plan to write in five or ten years.

It made me wonder if I have been writing the same story my whole life.

Which made me wonder if all stories are in some way the same story.

Which made me wonder why people keep buying books.

Which made me think that as a writer I should probably keep it to myself.

So, just between us, okay?

HOW NOT TO WRITE A SEQUEL

So many books now are written in series, and these efforts have unique challenges. I have discovered this over the last four years or so working on a sequel to my first novel *The Marriage of True Minds (Unbridled Books, 2008)*. This effort was a very different experience from writing the first book, easier in some ways, harder in others. If you are writing a sequel or a series, here are some questions you might ask yourself:

How will you tell the story?

Think about the way the previous book is structured, the architecture of the story. My first book had a nine-act structure. Should I continue with it? Mirror it. Or forget it and tell the next story independently? I chose to mirror the structure, as I felt it would work well for the story I was telling.

Who will be in the story?

This was one of the easier factors. I had a set of characters from the first book, and it was those characters that drew me back. So I made very few changes in the cast.

But the evolution of those characters was trickier than I expected. I felt in a way a responsibility to the characters, and to the readers who knew them. As I wrote, I was conscious about staying true to the original characters as the story continued.

Who will tell the story?

My first book used a complicated evolving point-of-view, introducing the reader to an expanded vision of the world with every chapter. It was not necessary for the second and would have over-complicated the telling. So I adopted instead mostly a limited third-person point of view.

Who will remember the story (part 1)?

There is a line in my book that says "memory is imagination in reverse." It had been years since I had read *The Marriage of True Minds.* I wondered if I should re-read it before starting on the new one.

I decided not to. I had a vision of the new book and energy to write it. I did not want to subvert or complicate that. However, during the editing process, I found myself continually checking back to the old text to confirm details. I found my recall level for these details at about 50/50. But then that is also my recall level for yesterday.

Who will remember the story (part 2)?

There was also the memory of the reader to consider. The first book was published ten years earlier. How much backstory was I going to have to add to the new one to make it work? And how much would that slow the new story?

I solved this by merging the two books into one: not a sequel, but a new work. My stories were short, less than 200 pages. And Unbridled Books graciously made the original text available for the purpose. I had to make some small changes in the first text, but nothing I think anyone (except me) will notice.

So in the end, I did not write a sequel at all. I wrote a book. In the process, I hope I created a better experience and a better value for the reader. But the process was similar. And if I write another sequel, or another book, I will be better prepared.

HOW PLAYS ARE WRITTEN

This is how my plays are written.

I was feeling pretty down today and not at all like writing, but I opened the laptop and looked at some of my works in progress. I usually have three or four things in the works, so I don't get bored with any one in particular.

I happened to open a one-act play I have been working on, thinking I would just see how far I had gotten the last time. I read the last line I had written and thought of a response. So I thought, well, I better write that down at least, or I will forget it. So I wrote it down. Then I thought of a response to that line, and I thought, well, I better write that down at least, or I will forget it. Ten pages later, I finally couldn't think of a response, so I stopped.

This is the kind of in-depth planning characteristic of my work.

THE MARK OF A WRITER

I wonder if the mark of a writer (in the ontological, not professional, sense) is that things seem better when you are writing, regardless of how they are. Or maybe it's that things are better when you are writing, regardless of how they seem.

THE LEXICON OF LOVE

I have often thought that the English language is deficient in that there are not enough words for the different kinds of love. We need a committee to classify them: I'm thinking maybe Shakespeare, Elizabeth Browning, and me (because I would like to meet Shakespeare and Elizabeth Browning).

But love lost is different, because it is the same. To reverse-paraphrase Tolstoy: each love is different; all lost loves are alike.

RANDOM THOUGHTS

I Keep Imagining

that someone will read what I write, if I keep imagining.

Possibility

The engine of creativity is the difference between what your life is and what you hoped it would be.

Hint Hint

When I feel anxious these days, which is often, I open my laptop and start to write. When the focus hits, the anxiety disappears. So I wonder if anxiety is really my brain's sneaky way of telling me to get back to work.

No Book is Finished

While someone is reading it.

Genius

Is the inability to not see.

Something Wants to be Written

A space builds outside.
A pressure grows inside.
Something wants to be written.
For which I am thankful.

A Theory

A corollary to the theory of Gnostic Fiction: Any book you have to read again to enjoy was not worth reading the first time.

Yours Truly

If someone mixes up your and you're, I say give them a break. If they mix up your and yore, intervention is required.

Just

Keep writing. He said.

Note to Myself

You have work to do.

Note to Myself

Start reading notes to myself.

It Came to Me in a Dream

Dreams are the language of the mind before language. The mind translates language into dream before the body translates dream into action.

My Favorite Word

Still.

Suspicion

I suspect reading the book I'm writing now will feel like spending several hours with that smart, funny, well-educated friend who won't shut up.

Write First

Think later.

I Wonder

If writing makes you aware or awareness makes you a writer.

We Need a New Word

Humane doesn't mean what it connotes.
Or is that humans don't.

Every Novel Should Begin with a Question

Usually “What was I thinking?”

How to Measure

A world is measured in miles, but a mind is measured in worlds.

The Tao of Sancho

Silence is joy.

Rules for Titles

If you can't say it five times fast, change it.
If you can say it ten times fast, it has changed you.

Spark Plugs and Synonyms

Suppose you had to explain to someone how a car works, but your explanation could use the parts of the car.

That is what writing about language is like.

Symbolically

One problem with a literary interpretation of drama is the misunderstanding of the way that symbols operate in performance.

There is No Rhyme to Reason

There is only reason to rhyme.

Always

Keep writing.
And rewriting.

The Book of Simon

Where is the Book of Simon? Where is Danny Simon on Writing Comedy? Surely that legacy will not go unpreserved.

Sleep

is the tenth muse.

Speareverse

Rosalind is a much more interesting character than Hamlet. Only Lear and Falstaff are as compelling in the Speareverse.

Headspace

When you are in the imaginative headspace of writing, it is so seductive to imagine having written.

All Stories are Sad

because they are stories.

My Writing Process

Make the bad things better.
Make the good things better.
Repeat.

Knowing and Understanding

There are words I have known for years that only now I understand.

My Favorite Bookstore

My favorite bookstore is the one with all the books I have dreamed of writing.

Failure

Every great work of art is a failure, because reaching for something greater is how it became great.

Exactly

The first draft of a play is a series of conversations in exactly the wrong order.

My Advice to Me

Do today's work.

Meaning

has too many meanings.

Watchwords

A few months ago, on the inside cover of my notebook, I wrote two phrases:

1) Patience.
2) Do it right.

Watchwords aren't easy.

If Writing is Enough

Enough of writing.

I Couldn't Write the Grief

So I had to write the gold.

BUMPER STICKERS FOR WRITERS

Fiction is a myth because the category implies that there is something other than fiction.

Literary fiction is a metamyth.

Literary fiction is what you read today and remember tomorrow.

Literary fiction is what will be read 100 years from now, but not now.

The best thing about writing literary fiction is that you send a thought out into the Universe and you never know who's not going to read it.

POOH'S GUIDE TO MAKING UP STORIES

Sometimes I think the highest point of western literature was reached in 1928 with the publication of *The House at Pooh Corner*. Here are Pooh's rules for stories. As Told To, of course.

1. Find your Hundred Acre Wood.
2. Always put on the Big Boots before the Adventure.
3 Do not use words that only Owl can understand.
4. Every Kanga has a Roo.
5. Doing nothing is something.
6. Hum if you feel like it.
7. Sometimes Heffalumps are not.
8 Always know where Christopher Robin is.
9. Don't forget the hunny.

10. Ten is too many.

MAKES SENSE TO ME

Purpose requires meaning.
Meaning requires understanding.
Understanding requires language.
So for now, my purpose is language.
Which for a writer is very convenient.

OPERATORS ARE STANDING BY

You've written your will.

Planned your funeral.

Why leave your last words to chance?

We at FinalScribe offer an amazing selection of last words designed to convey the essence of your life wisdom in one perfect phrase. Our highly trained associates are standing now by to help you choose the ideal testimonial for your life. Here are just a few of our most popular choices:

"Nevermore, nevertheless."

"On the whole, I prefer taxes."

"Who knew?"

Or, for a small percentage of your estate (plus shipping and handling), we will customize your last words to your specifications. Philosophical. Poignant. Funny. Ecstatic. Our terminologists (graduates all of prestigious MFA Writing Programs) can match your mood to the last syllable.

For an additional fee, we can record and time your last words, or even hire an actor to say them for you. From Broadway favorites to Classical soliloquies, our closers are experts at making your death seem as profound and moving to your audience as it is to you.

Why wait?

There's no time like...well, there's no time.

WHAT DOES IT SAY ABOUT ME

That I prefer *Middlemarch* and *The Age of Innocence* to *The Sun Also Rises* and *This Side of Paradise*?

That I prefer Nineteenth century writers to the Twentieth? Maybe.

Does it say that I prefer women writers to men? Possibly.

That I prefer a writer who writes like me? Definitely not.

I wonder if the reason is the latter two were written by young writers, while the first two were written by mature writers. Hemingway was 27, Fitzgerald was 25. Eliot was 52, Wharton was 58.

Maybe the flashy characters and unconventional (for the time) styles do not interest me as much as the delicate perceptions and compelling characters of the more experienced story tellers.

Further research may be needed...

THE CIRCLE OF ACTING

The feeling shows itself:

First through the body.

Then through the mind.

Then through the voice.

Then again through the body.

YOU KNOW, THAT FEELING

That feeling when you're writing a scene and everything goes away and you go away and nothing exists but the characters in the scene and you come back to yourself and it's an hour later.

And you're glad to go away and glad to come back and you hope you can go again and you know you can because the characters will take you there.

That’s a good feeling.

THE COMPETENT NOVELIST

I think that the only competent playwright we have is Shakespeare. The only competent poet is Dickinson. The only competent composers are Bach and Mozart. The only competent artist is Van Gogh. The only competent sculptor is Michelangelo.

There are no competent novelists. The novel as an art has not yet arrived at the point where there could be. But we feel the gravity of it as it approaches the planet, to shatter us.

I find hope in this. if we can manage to last, to progress, and to understand, the greatness of the past is only the barest competence compared to what we might one day create. The world seems always waiting for its competent novelist.

And let me add, the Vienna Finger is the only competent cookie.

THE TEN GREATEST SCIENCE FICTION NOVELS

By greatest, I suppose I mean the highest achievement in both imaginative scope and literary execution. If you prefer, you could replace the word greatest with favorite and you would still be accurate. Here are my choices:

Childhood's End, Arthur C. Clarke
Dune, Frank Herbert
Stranger in a Strange Land, Robert Heinlein
A Canticle for Leibowitz, Walter M. Miller Jr.
20,000 Leagues under the Sea, Jules Verne
City, Clifford D. Simak
Dhalgren, Samuel R. Delaney
The Left Hand of Darkness, Ursula LeGuin
The End of Eternity – Isaac Asimov
To Your Scattered Bodies Go, Phillip Jose Farmer

So that's my list. If you don't have one, this may be a good place to start exploring.

Methodology: I have included only books I have read (usually many times). I have arbitrarily excluded such excellent series as the *Lensman* series by E.E. Doc Smith, the *Foundation* series by Isaac Asimov, and the *Space Trilogy* by C. S. Lewis, though I have included the first book of the *Riverworld* series because I feel it can stand alone. I have also excluded excellent novels that I consider primarily social critiques such as *Slaughterhouse-5, 1984, Fahrenheit 451, A Clockwork Orange*, and books I considered primarily fantasy. I have also generally excluded linked stories, though you could argue both *City* and *Childhood's End* would qualify (I don't).

THE NINE BEST PLAYS WRITTEN IN ENGLISH

Here is my list of the nine best plays written originally in English:

A Midsummer Night's Dream
King Lear
Our Town
As You Like It
Henry IV (Parts 1 & 2)
Twelfth Night
The Importance of Being Earnest
The Odd Couple
A Long Day's Journey into Night

I could not decide on a tenth.

Waiting for Godot was originally written in French. *Hamlet* wanders too much, depends too much on one relatively annoying if unique character. *Othello*, no. You could make a case for *Macbeth*. *The Lion in Winter*–maybe, maybe. *Death of a Salesman*–fine play but not top ten.

Nothing from the twenty-first century that I have read or seen makes the list, but give it a few more decades. Something great must be coming.

AS I RECALL

A memoir should be like a good first date.

It shouldn't tell you everything.

And it shouldn't make you cry.

SHAKESPEARE IS POINTLESS

My plays have points, purposes for which I write, meanings I hope to convey. Possibly clever, possibly profound, possibly worth the effort to discern. And possibly not. Nevertheless, they point.

Shakespeare's plays are pointless; they are beyond point. They are not text. They are theater. They are in performance. Lear is not about fathers and daughters. Hamlet is not about, well, anything. Hamlet is. Lear is. When it is. When it isn't, it is not.

Someday I would like to write something that was pointless. But it is probably pointless for me to try.

FEAST

I saw a pair of vultures flying almost too high to see, so graceful, gliding, now and then a brief dip of the wings. I thought that it was an apt metaphor for being a writer, soaring aloft, yet descending occasionally to feast on the dead.

ACTION, PLOT, STORY

Action is what happens.

Plot is why it happens.

Story is why it matters.

ZERO SLOPE

Zero Tolerance and the Slippery Slope are rhetorical devices, intended to short-circuit intelligent decisions rather than promote them.

I have zero tolerance for the slippery slope and avoid the slippery slope of zero tolerance.

Or maybe just this once is okay.

TALENTS

I sometimes think the only true talents in writing are:

> Knowing what's good.
> Knowing what's better.

The rest is just time and work.

STEPHEN'S WAY

I like to read and I'm not put usually off by difficult books. I have read *War and Peace*, *The Brothers Karamazov*, much of Faulkner, most of Joyce. But there are a few books that I have never been able to finish, and so far as I can tell they have nothing in common.

The first is *Godel, Escher, Bach* by Douglas Hofstader. It came out a few years after I graduated and was a combination of two things that for me (and possibly only for me) are inseparably linked: philosophy and comedy. I have never been able to read the entire book, mostly because at least once each page I have to stop and think, and once my brain is so activated it seldom circles back to the beginning point. I was lucky if I remembered to mark my place.

The second book is *The Magic Mountain* by Thomas Mann. I started this one based on the recommendation of Joseph Campbell, who ranked Mann with James Joyce as the great mytho-centric writers of the Twentieth century. With Mann, you have some choices. I picked *The Magic Mountain* because *Death in Venice* was too short, *Buddenbrooks* (reputedly his masterpiece) was too long, so *The Magic Mountain* seemed just right.

Plus it had magic in the title, though as I discovered there were no elves or wizards, at least not as far as I got. I was enjoying *The Magic Mountain* despite its fantasy-barren nature, but life intervened, the book was packed away, and to date it has not been found. Though I did get one nice poem out it. Still I hope to find my copy one day and begin again.

The third book is Marcel Proust's *Swann's Way*, the initial volume in Proust's *À la recherche du temps perdu*, which is sometimes poetically translated as *Remembrance of Things Past* and oddly translated as *In Search of Lost Time*, which sounds like a story about someone who couldn't find their watch. Proust was a contemporary of both Joyce and Mann. Proust and Joyce met once in a famous encounter where each complained about his health and excused himself (true writerish behavior).

I had a copy of *Remembrance of Things Past* that somehow resurfaced, which I took as a sign that I should try again. Previously I had made it to the scene with the tea and madeleine, and then gave up, possibly because it made me hungry, though more likely because I felt I had done my duty. The translation I had was the original English translation by C. K. Scott Moncrief, which was regarded as the standard. But after a few pages of this, I decided to switch to a later translation by Lydia Davis. I don't know which is more Proustean, but Ms. Davis work was slightly livelier and I stuck with it.

In theory I could read it in French. I took eight years of French and can speak but not really pronounce several words at least. I suspect the book is better in the original, and I have the same suspicion about Mann in German and Dante in Italian and Homer in Greek. But for now, and likely forever, I will have to rely on the wonderful work of translators, who so remarkably devote years of their lives to other people's words.

At this reporting, I am 150 pages into *Swann's Way* and I am pretty sure that other than tea and madeleines nothing has happened. But I must say it is not happening marvelously and I can't wait to see what doesn't happen next.

Author's Note: As of this writing, I have finished *The Magic Mountain* (had to buy a new copy) and *Swann's Way*, both marvelous if not easy, and I am about half way through *Gödel, Escher, Bach*, which so far is less marvelous but completely fascinating.

So I will need some new books to have never read. If you have suggestions, let me know.

Gravity's Rainbow seems promising.

WORTH FAILING AT

I finished rereading *Ulysses* by James Joyce again a few days ago and have been pondering. Today's thought:

> Strong writing.
> Brilliant construction.
> Magnificent failure.
> Magnificent in what it attempts.
> Failure in that it sacrifices understanding for expression.

But worth failing at.

WRITING WHAT IS WRITTEN

At some point in the last century we began to conflate the expressions:

Great author.
Great writer.

Yet I often think that the two are, if not exclusive, at least opposed. How we write is less important than what. Saying can get in the way of what is said.

SPOILER ALERT

There are only two valid book reviews:

> I liked it.
> I didn't like it.

My review of Julian Barnes *The Sense of an Ending* is: I liked it.

THE DAY THE STORIES FAIL

I've been binge-watching Game of Thrones for the who-knows-how-manyieth time. And in the process, mainly while the credits roll or I'm fast forwarding through the parts that I don't enjoy as much, I have been wondering why I watch this, why it is so enthralling, and why I can watch it for the who-knows-how-manyieth time and still find it enthralling.

In the *Biographia Literaria*, Coleridge wrote about the willing suspension of disbelief:

"My endeavours should be directed to persons and characters supernatural, or at least romantic, yet so as to transfer from our inward nature a human interest and a semblance of truth sufficient to procure for these shadows of imagination that willing suspension of disbelief for the moment, which constitutes poetic faith."

Interesting. But I don't think that's quite it. It's not a suspension of disbelief. It is belief. And it is not willing.

There is nothing of choice about it. We are enthralled, or we have enthralled ourselves. But it is not magic but neurology that captures us.

I believe stories work because of the imperative of belief. Deep down in the animal brain (which, let's be honest, is almost all of it), there is an inability to understand that stories, whether on the page or on the screen, are not real. In some small part of the brain, we know, but we can't overcome the other part. Or we forget about it as the story unfolds.

Yet there is a difference between stories and reality, if that exists anymore. There is some understanding that stories, real or not we can't say, are not happening to us. This gives us the safety to enjoy, to experience the terror and heartbreak and grandeur without the need to run to safety.

One day, far in the future, I imagine, we or our descendants, or the descendants of whatever species are left, will lose this disability, this imperative to believe will disappear. Brains will automatically distinguish between what is real and what is not. Stories, all of them, will fail.

These lucky creatures, unable to see the world other than it is, will not understand the power our stories held over us. And they will wonder in disbelief why we writers spent our lives creating them.

CAMPBELLING

In *The Importance of Being Earnest* by Oscar Wilde, Algernon describes the phenomenon of *Bunburying*, in which he uses the excuse of visiting his sick friend Bunbury to avoid social functions. I have a similar phenomenon, though I do not use it to avoid so much as to inspire.

My escape is *Campbelling*, in which I dive into one of the remarkable books of Joseph Campbell, Master of the Endless Domains of Comparative Mythology. I dive into one of his books and seldom fail to come out the other end with something creative brewing. You can see the aftereffects of *The Hero's Journey* in both *The Marriage of True Minds* and *The Marriage Gift*.

My current endeavor is Campbell's *Oriental Mythology* (the comparison of Biblical patriarchs and Sumerian Kings is fascinating). But my favorite is *Creative Mythology*, where he explores Medieval Romance (once of my permanent obsessions).

I also go Shelleying sometimes.

But that's another story.

Author's Note: I finally had to order a new copy of *Creative Mythology*. My old one has been read so often that it fell apart.

THE FLOW OF ART

There used to be a bookstore maybe twenty miles from me called Daedalus Books that sold publishers remainders or overstock at good prices. They always had an unusual selection in stock, lots of art and drama and philosophy and other subjects that are tucked away in the back of larger bookstores (if there are any left). Sadly, the Daedalus physical store has morphed into an online version, as so many have.

Years ago (I'm not sure of the number but probably more than some and less than many), I purchased a book there called *The Flow of Art*. I didn't look at it then: but it sounded like a book on the philosophy of art, or the mechanisms of art, or something equally esoteric. My reading was delayed until this year, when I finally rescued it from the bottom shelf of a bookcase.

As it turned out, it was neither philosophy or how-to, but a compilation of art reviews by critic Henry McBride from his lofty position as the art critic for the New York Sun newspaper from the turn of the Twentieth century onward. Fortunately, Mr. McBride had the opportunity to observe some of the most compelling and exciting art and artists that century produced. Some of them I have heard of: Picasso, Braque, Matisse, Rodin, and so forth. Many others are new to me, and will provide many fine hours of research and appreciation.

McBride's contemporaneous viewpoint is fascinating, and his intimate engagement with both art and artist (and other critics) is enlightening and entertaining. But what astonishes me most in these pieces is the quality of the prose.

Voice is the rarest of qualities in a writer. You can write a good book without it (Shakespeare had it, Marlowe didn't; Woolf had it, Joyce didn't, and so on), but you have to work much harder.

McBride's prose has voice, unique and simple and full of good humor regarding the world he reports on and the reporter himself. He invites us all into this remarkable world with such ease and pleasure, as though he were sharing a thought over an espresso (probably in a café with Stein and Cezanne in the background).

If you have the chance to join him for a cup or two, I highly recommend it.

THE EXPRESSIVE MIND

Contemporary cognitive scientists and philosophers tend to regard the human mind as hierarchical, with consciousness and subconscious functions, and thinking as the highest achievement. A better model might be the mind as an expressive organ, with all modes of expression interacting in the mind on a more or less equal plane. These modes of expression might be thought of as:

Symbolic expression
Emotional expression
Image expression
Numerical expression
Spatial expression
Duration expression.

See, I didn't sleep through those classes on Phenomenology.

SUZABOOL

When I was very young, post picture book but pre-Tom Swift, the library in my town was housed in a converted Victorian mansion. The children's section was a small rectangular room just off the vestibule, maybe a coatroom in its heyday. The shelves were appropriately low and multi-colored, and I would run for them directly whenever I was released from my mother's grasp.

Somewhere on those shelves in some year buried in my memory, I found a wonderful book that I only vaguely remember, but have vaguely remembered for half a century.

I don't know the title. There were three professors with funny names like Whichwhat or Whohow, and a maid named Suzabool. And I think there was something about a leaf.

I would love to find that book again. But even more, I would love to write a book that someone would remember for fifty years, even if only vaguely.

ELEVEN WRITING RULES FOR THE REST OF US

I read recently that two million books were published last year. And more will be published this year, and more next year. Knowing how hard it is for me to write one book, I think that's amazing.

Yet in all that literary cacophony, how is a writer to break through? I have no idea. We can try if we like. But I suspect that 1, 999,000 of us will be disappointed.

I have seen writing rules and suggestions from famous writers. But here are my writing rules for the rest of us:

Take your time.
Ignore trends.
Work hard, but not every day.
Don't write what you know.
Don't write what anyone else knows either.
Try for greatness.
Don't settle.

Listen to criticism but trust yourself.

Publish carefully sometime.

Write the book only you can write.

I have a quote from Marcus Aurelius over my desk. It is my 11th rule:

"If you work at that which is before you, following right reason seriously, vigorously, calmly, without allowing anything else to distract you, but keeping your divine part pure, as if you should be bound to give it back immediately; if you hold to this, expecting nothing, fearing nothing, but satisfied with your present activity according to nature, and with heroic truth in every word and sound which you utter, you will live happy. And there is no man who is able to prevent this."

Good Stoic advice for emperors and writers.

STORY AND CONFLICT

Most books on writing novels (or any kind of narrative) tell you that you need to have conflict to drive the story and keep the reader's interest. Screenwriting texts make an imperative out of escalating the stakes for the protagonist.

Conflict is important to a story. But stories have an inherent, and inherently sufficient, conflict built into them. The essential conflict is between the story and the reader. In the trade, this dramatic conflict is technically referred to as 'what happens next?'.

And that's all I have to say about that.

THAT IS THE QUESTION

Three questions:

How many writers keep getting better until the end?

Or maybe, how few?

And why?

Shakespeare is in the first category; the *Tempest* is pretty wonderful. Though the problem plays are problems, you can feel the attempt to reach through to something new.

Chekov possibly.

Cervantes. I don't know. Haven't read the later works.

Help me out here.

Rimbaud is cheating, since he gave it all up early. Not a bad plan in all.

Hardy switched to poetry for the last 20 years or so of his life. Also not a bad plan.

Buddies Truman Capote and Harper Lee don't count. Capote could never finish another book after *In Cold Blood.* Lee could finish only the one.

Joyce disappeared into *Finnegans* and never reappeared.

Yeats – better and better until the end.

Who am I missing?

Thomas Mann? I have only read *The Magic Mountain*. Yet, unlikely.

So. Shakespeare and Yeats.

Does genius require a physical vigor, or emotional, or both, that is lost over time?

Sorry, that's four questions.

WATCHWORDS

A few months ago, on the inside cover of my notebook, I wrote two phrases:

1) Patience.
2) Do it right.

Watchwords aren't easy.

I WILL WRITE NO MORE FOREVER

These words have been circling in my mind for the last week or so. They are a paraphrase of the last words of Chief Joseph of the Nez Pierce explaining his decision to finally surrender. It is a searing speech you should read, if you haven't.

The catalyst for me was the recent article in The New Yorker about the struggles and eventual suicide of author David Foster Wallace. But the thought, the question, has been with me for a while, since I finished my last book I guess.

I have been wondering if there is a time for a writer to stop. To say I have written what has been given to me and now I will be silent. To say: I will write no more forever.

APPLES IN THE DARK

People sometimes ask me where my stories come from. For me it is like picking apples in the dark.

You reach.

Sometimes they're there.

Sometimes they're not.

And sometimes they just fall on your head.

TO MY BIOGRAPHER

Please leave out the boring parts.
That's my philosophy in Reading, in Writing, and in Life.
Okay, not so much in Life.
So it may be a short book.
Essays are good.
Or Haiku...

APPENDIX A: A PHENOMENOLOGY OF ART

Author's Note: Presented for your entertainment: my undergraduate philosophy thesis (with a few edits)

Why?

The first question to ask on entering into a phenomenology of art is: why should we attempt one? At all? Ever?

What is there specifically about phenomenology that would make such a venture worthwhile? There are many other approaches to the philosophy of art. Why depart from these as a basis?

Here is the answer: these classical approaches to the philosophy of art have, in the more than two millennia since Aristotle, proved grossly inadequate. They made a bad start in the first place by assuming that art imitates nature. While they have recovered somewhat from this misadventure, they still tend to flounder in their own terminology.

One advantage of phenomenology is the process of aside preconceptions and misconceptions and examining the phenomena itself. In general, art seems to have a duality at its heart. Or actually two: dual dualities, which are very difficult to join into any coherent and comprehensible theory.

Considered in itself, art seems to exist to be experienced. There is something about art which seems to jump out at the viewer, which separates the work of art from the world around it. Art exists to show itself; indeed so dominant is this characteristic that it might be said to be ontological in nature. However, the fact that art has ontological characteristics, that it has characteristics in and for itself, causes problems when you try to connect it with the other side of the two-fold nature of art.

Art is the most human of artifacts. It communicates more about humanity than any other of man's creations. It deals with his problems and emotions in the tragic, with his intellectual apprehensions in the comic, and in a more primordial sense, in some modern art especially, with the nature of man's perception of the world itself. Any philosophy of art should encompass not only the characteristics which art exhibits in itself, but also the intimate relation which art shares with humanity.

There is a fundamental problem here, one which might be said to have caused considerable difficulties in previous philosophies of art. Though it may be a problem more with philosophers than with philosophies.

If you start out with art as it is in itself, then it is difficult to switch mid-stream and turn to art in its relation to man, and vice versa. For one thing, as we have noted, the terminology tends to be stretched too far, trying to do things for which it was not originally designed. The problem is in tying together radically different conceptual schemes with the same, coherent terminology. This is where phenomenology can help.

According to Heidegger, the word 'phenomenon' has two seemingly very different meanings. The first meaning of phenomenon is "that which shows itself". The phenomenon is the manifest, that which appears to us. In this sense, art is the quintessential phenomenon, in that its very existence involves showing itself. The second meaning of phenomenon is ‘semblance’, or that which it shows itself to be. Phenomenology is the methodology which joins the two.

Begin with things as they appear. All things appear to us within the structures of our consciousness. By understanding these structures and how they affect the phenomena as given, and by adequate description of these phenomena as they show themselves, or in my terms, how they behave in our experience of them, we can derive a knowledge of the ontological characteristics of the things in themselves. As Heidegger says:

Everything depends on our seeing how what is designated by the first signification (phenomena as that which shows itself) and by the second (phenomena as semblance) are structurally related.

By starting with art in its relation to man, we can derive knowledge of how art exists in itself, and lots of other good things besides. We can unite the seeming dual nature of art through phenomenology.

What?

Now, having determined the need for attempting a phenomenology of art, let's turn to our description of art. Before we do that, however, we must attempt what Husserl calls the époque, the transcendental reduction. In this transition, what we are actually doing is trying to remove all unexamined presumptions, so that we are able look freshly and clearly at the phenomenon. Actually, it's a useful method for many areas in life.

I don't think I'm fooling anybody by saying that we must at this point do this or that move in the methodology. You all know that if I hadn't done it already, I wouldn't be writing it now. As a matter of fact, I never really made any transcendental reduction. However, I was an artist, and formed my basic opinions on art, long before I read any philosophy of art. So you might say that in my innocence (or ignorance) I approximated a transcendental reduction.

Given that I have performed such a reduction, you might find it strange that I seem to rely rather heavily on other philosophers for my description. I really did think of taking all the credit for myself, except that those other philosophers said much of what I wanted to say so much better than I could that it seemed very disrespectful of me to even consider such an action. So I let them in and gave them credit. However, everything in the following phenomenological description has been confirmed time and again by my experience as an artist and a serious student of art.

Art appears to us in an amazing variety of forms, shapes and sizes. The range of art stretches from sounds (music, poetry) to colors (painting) to figures (sculpture). In fact, anything that can be sensed can be turned into art. No wonder art theorists have had such difficult times arriving at a definition of art. The problem of a definition of art, whether we can define it at all, will have to wait till the end of the paper, when we have the conceptual tools to deal with it adequately. Yet, there do seem to be certain fundamental characteristics which are common to all art. We have touched on one already; all art seems to have sensible qualities. As obvious as this may seem to everybody, there are theorists who would disagree in some sense, saying that the art exists in a sort of virtual image. But, since this question presumes an certain epistemological and ontological resolutions, I think it is beyond the scope of our phenomenology.

A second characteristic that all art seems to share is framing. In theater, this effect is accomplished by lighting and the proscenium, in music, by the silence before the performance, and in painting by the physical frame. Framing separates the work of art from the ordinary functions of the world.

Art doesn't function in the world in the same way as ordinary things do. Art resists categorization in the usual functional pattern. Certainly, you could hit some-one over the head with a statue, but it would not be functioning in that example "as art". Rudolpho, in Puccini's La Boheme, does not write his five-act tragedy just so he can burn it. Ultimately, art has no function but is an end in itself

Art does appear to have a function, in a sense: the function of communication. Yet, certainly, the function of communication could not be said to be the sole property of art. We communicate in other important ways as well.

Take poetry. What is there about poetry, or artistic language, which separates it from ordinary declarative prose: discursive language?

Consider first the way in which discursive language operates.

Close the door.

The meaning of each of the words in the sentence above is completely independent of the other words in the sentence. You might argue that some words can be either nouns or verbs depending on their position, and that close means different things when you say 'close the door' than when you say 'the close door'. Yet this is just the peculiarity of using the same symbol for different words. In any case, once the sentence has been written down the meanings of the words are independent of one another and the process of discovering the meaning is roughly equivalent to a simple mechanical process. If You know that Close is a command to perform a certain process or function and you know that The is an article directing you to the noun Door, which is that rectangular thing hanging by the hole in the wall, then you can put them all together and calulate, or otherwise mechanically arrive at, the meaning close-the-door. It is all very simple and efficient.

Artistic language does not work in the same way as discursive language. Consider the opening line from Keats' *Ode on a Grecian Urn*:

Thou still unravished bride of quietness,

The meaning of this line can never be determined by a simple mechanical process, nor could the next:

Beauty is Truth, truth beauty,

The above line is not simply an identity statement but, taken in its historical context, it is the identity of non-identicals. It is a paradoxical statement whose meaning is not mechanically determinable. We could not reduce the determination of the meaning of the line to an arithmetic, nor logical, nor systematicl operation, because the form of the line is fundamentally different from that of a discursive line. Even aside from the artist's techniques, or tricks, involved in each of these lines, tricks which ambiguate the sentence, still you could not determine mechanically the meaning of the line because the meaning of the terms in the line are not independent as they are in discursive language. Rather, they are the product of the inter-relations between the terms in their particular relations. The line presents itself as a unity, a gestalt, thus ultimately transcending any form of analysis.

How does the unity of the line prevent analysis? Since the process of analysis consists of breaking into discrete parts and then re-relating them to determine meaning, it is not applicable to the poetic line. Once you break the poetic line into discrete units, you destroy the meaning each of those discrete units had, since that meaning was not independent but dependent on the inter-relations within the line. Destroy the unity of the poem and you distort its meaning. This is what the poet means when he says that the meaning of the poem is the poem. The meaning of the poem is unstatable in terms other than the poem itself (this is of course true only for the pure lyric poem. Epic and dramatic poems bring in other elements which, although they are by no means contradictory, tend to cloud the issue and so will not be dealt with here.)

Notice from what we have said already that the rational processes are associated with the discursive forms of language and the irrational (in the sense of ambiguous and paradoxical) contents are associated with artistic languages. So it would seem that artistic language differs from discursive language in content as well as form, if indeed content and form are even separable from one another. This theory coincides nicely with Suzanne Langer's description of the content of art, when she says:

> *There is a great deal of experience which is knowable not only as immediate, formless, meaningless impact, but as one aspect of the intricate web of life, vet defies discursive formulation, and therefore, objective expression.*

This type of human experience, which Langer (the most under-rated philosopher of the twentieth century) calls the life of feeling, would seem to be the source of the content of art. However, we need not go into the content of art too deeply here, so long as we recognize the general antipathy of art to discursive language, both in form and content, as this will become important later. So in order to explain this antipathy more clearly, we can theorize a possible historical account of the development of these two expressive forms.

We are aware that both art and language grew out of a need to formulate experience, and then to communicate that experience. (Communication was the essential though still secondary need.) Yet the purposes of the two forms were and are quite distinct. Discursive language was developed to help more efficiently communicate survival information. In approaching this goal, the tool of discursive language developed its own powerful methods, methods which in part we have already examined. Notice for example that if someone yelled at us:

You are going to be trampled by an elephant

most of us would take evasive action, whereas if he had couched his statement in metaphorical, terms, we would very likely end up in the hospital. While this whole line of reasoning may have dubious philosophical value, I hope it may clarify the distinction between artistic and discursive language, because the distinction is a crucial point in our understanding of art and the ontology of the world.

In any case, we can see that the meaning of a work of art is a very different thing from the meaning of an ordinary sentence. A work of art can only be said to have a meaning in a very limited sense. A work has no meaning outside itself and the meaning is communicated only through the experience of the work.

In this quality we find one of the primary values of the work of art. Art is valuable because it enriches our experience by communicating things outside the frame of our average existence. Yet, here we seem to find another universal value of art. The experience of art is much more vital and intense than most of our everyday experiences. The American philosopher, John Dewey, thought this to be the primary value of art:

> *It is mere ignorance that leads then to the supposition that connection of art and esthetic perception with experience is a lowering of their significance and dignity. Experience in the degree in which it is experience is heightened vitality. Instead of signifying being shut up within one's own private feelings and sensations, it signifies active and alert commerce with the world; at its height it signifies complete interpenetration of self and the world of objects and events.*

Art for Dewey is valuable mostly because it is a form of heightened and enriched experience. In some sense, we can account for this vitality on the basis of the form and content of art. Yet, in order to fully understand the vitality of the work of art, we must examine the way in which we experience the work of art. We must investigate the experience, and therefore the structures of consciousness itself.

How?

In the notion of reflecting on the structures of consciousness, we might be somewhat at a loss as to how to begin. Do we depend on essential insights, as Husserl and probably Heidegger did? Or do we attempt to argue back from our own perceptions, as Kant did, to reach the structures of the transcendental ego?

While there are arguments for both sides, we really must do both. For to have an experience is to have at least a basic intuition of the structure of that experience. It is absurd to presume an intuition of the conditions of experience independent of that experience, or to presume that we can deduce from that experience the entire structure of the experience without having any clue as to how to proceed in our deduction. The experience is not distinct from its structure. Therefore, to have an experience is to have an intuition of the structure of that experience. All that is left for us is to make that intuition clear and explicit within the realm of our phenomenological pursuit.

The basic intuition of phenomenology is that consciousness is always consciousness of something. We never have a pure experience without an object for that consciousness. Consciousness, in other words, invariably intends an object, is in relation to an object. The structure of consciousness must therefore be the nature or essence of that relation. Therefore, an understanding of the structures of consciousness is necessarily an understanding of the relations which consciousness can enter into.

Obviously, the types of relations which consciousness can enter into will be limited by the types of relations that exist. So, for a time, let's turn to a metaphysical investigation of relations. At first glance, there would seem to be thousands of types of relations that consciousness could enter into, and millions of different relations in all. Yet in reality, all these can be reduced to two basic relations, which we may call by the classical metaphysical concepts of the class as many and the class as one.

These two concepts embody the two primordial relations that exist and form in themselves the basis for all metaphysics. The misunderstanding and misuse of the concepts embodied in these relations are responsible for most of the difficulties of metaphysics from Aristotle to Aquinas and on up through Russell. This is not the place for a discussion of their application to other metaphysical problems, but this applicability can easily be deduced once they are properly understood.

In considering the class as a relation, simply think of it in terms of the objects which it joins, the constituents of the class. In phenomenological terms, consider one of the constituents of the class to be consciousness and the other or others, the objects.

In the concept of the class as many, the class is something abstracted from the objects, usually due to a rational recognition of a common quality. For instance, 'human' is a notion abstracted from a set of individual human beings. The notion is separable and distinct from the individuals from which it was abstracted, which causes substantial problems when we try to say that Socrates is a human being, but that's beside the point. The class as many is the relating of distinct individuals.

In the concept of the class as one, nothing is abstracted, nothing is taken away, nothing is outside of the relation. The individuals exist, creating another individual. Consider what this means to the notion of the individual. So far, we have considered that when we perceive, we actually perceive individuals and individuals (or particles) only. Now we see that what constitutes an individual is not some form of indivisible wholeness; rather, what constitutes an individual is the relation. This notion of absolutely indivisible particles has been by far the most harmful in the history of metaphysics. One would have thought it would have gone out of use after Aristotle's destruction of Zeno's arguments, but instead it has pervaded our metaphysics and, with Hume, our epistemology. That the notion of sense-data is actually logically absurd doesn't seem to have bothered any of them.

No matter what Hume says, we recognize individuals by recognizing the relation that constitutes that individual. Consider the problems that the notion of absolute particularity has caused in the field of quantum physics. Once we conceived of sub-atomic particles, it was inevitable that we should have to run into the problem of the Heisenberg uncertainty principle. The evolution to field theory and string theory is simply an attempt to formulate the world in terms of relations rather than particles. The relation of the class as one is the basic, primordial relation of the universe. The class as many is a man-made relation which our consciousness has forced upon the world; certainly it has its uses, but to imagine that it constitutes the true nature of reality is simply to perpetuate the metaphysical problems which Aristotle encountered.

How can we apply these notions of the class or relation as many and as one to consciousness? Well, in fact, consciousness, as you might expect, already includes this two-fold notion of relation. These two relations constitute the structure of consciousness. Yet we need not here develop an entirely new philosophy or phenomenology to formulate this structure of consciousness. Martin Heidegger, in his book, Being and Time, has already done so for us.

In *Being and Time*, Heidegger attempts to derive a basis for a fundamental ontology. He imagines an entity, Dasein, for which being is at issue. Dasein , which I refer to as people, is Heidegger's crystallization of Husserl's transcendental reduction. This entity dasein exists in the world and has dealings with objects in the world. Heidegger characterizes these dealings in the world in two ways, ready-to-hand or present-to-hand. These characterizations are both ways in which the object appears to dasein and an attitude which dasein has towards the objects. In short, dasein is related to objects in in these two ways. Yet, these two ways are still the structures of consciousness, which Heidegger gives ontological status mostly, I think, because he wants to avoid any realist presuppositions in his fundamental ontology. This is understandable because phenomenology in general likes to stay away from questions of idealism and realism.

Ready-to-hand is the way in which the world generally appears to us. We approach things in the world in terms of their use or function. They exist as objects, separate from us and considered only in so far as they aid us in achieving our goals. The totality, the structure of dasein's average, every day, in-order-to relations constitutes the worldhood of the world. This structure is the reason why the world appears to us as such. This structure of ready-to-hand is actually the relation which I have described above a the class as many. It is the relation of two things as absolutely distinct. In order to use things, we must look at them as objects existing outside us, separate from us. Thus, we developed rationality as a conscious method of dealing with the world in this way, and we developed discursive language and, in a purified form, logic, to enable us to describe these relations. Both discursive language and ready-to-hand relations are based on the relation of the class as many; look back and see how each of the words in the example of discursive language is absolutely distinct, its meaning is independent. The clear association of rationality and the rational processes with the ready-to-hand relation can be seen to be the result of their unified metaphysical basis.

There is another type of relation or attitude or structure of consciousness within which Dasein encounters objects in the world. Whenever an object does not act in a normal functional manner, whenever it does not act as a tool or instrument for accomplishing Dasein's goals, the object breaks the in-order-to structures that constitute Dasein's ordinary world. The object then exists for Dasein in the present-to-hand mode. In this mode, the object is seen as an end in itself, an entity which confronts Dasein. The mode of present-to-hand corresponds directly with the relation of the class as one. The other characteristics of this relation as it appears in consciousness would not seem to be important here, which is good, because I haven't been able to work them out coherently- yet. The relation of the present-to-hand to art will be dealt with in part III.

Heidegger contends that the relation of ready-to-hand is more primordial than that of present-at-hand. He says this because he wants to maintain that the ready-to-hand is the source of our vague, average understanding of being, which is the foundation of his fundamental ontology. He also wants to do this because he wrongly associates theoretical knowledge with the present-to-hand. As we have seen, it is the ready-to-hand that is associated with the rational, with theoretical knowledge. Heidegger is equally unfounded in his other contentions of the primordiality of the ready-to-hand.

Consider Heidegger's ideas on language. Heidegger says that we have a ready-to-hand knowledge of language, a knowledge which is not understandable in explicit and theoretical terms; for instance, we do not first learn languages by rules, nor can we reduce a language to simple rules. Here he misconstrues; to attempt to explain language in terms of component function (i.e. grammatical rules) is to explain it in terms of an inter-related system of functionality, which is the definition not of present-to-hand but of the ready-to-hand. If this contention is correct, then our knowledge of language, and of being, does not extend from the ready-to-hand but from the present-to-hand. Language exists for us as an entity, a whole, a gestalt. The totality of language is the source of our ready-to-hand knowledge of language; and our knowledge of that totality, that organic whole, is present-to-hand.

The same sort of objection can be made regarding to Heidegger's contention that since our average understanding of the world is of the world of the ready-to-hand, that therefore the ready-to-hand is more primordial than the present-to-hand. Despite the fact that the world-ness of the world is made up of the ready-to-hand objects, we still know these objects in their organic totality, their structure of inter-relations, and so our knowledge of the world must be present-to-hand. From this, and from the fact which we saw earlier, that the only relation which exists between objects in the world is that of the present-to-hand, we can see that the relation of present-at-hand must be the most primordial.

Let’s now at some of the characteristics of the relation of present-at-hand. In the first place, phenomena which are present-to-hand are more immediate. We see them without the mediation of a goal directed intentionality. They are ends in themselves and not merely means as they would be seen in the ready-to-hand. Also, they are seen without the mediation of conceptualization, since rationality and conceptualization exist primarily in the ready-to-hand. Conceptualization, which is the co-product of discursive language, separates the phenomenon from consciousness in so far as it mediates and even determines experience. Phenomena which are encountered as present-to-hand do not have this mediating conceptuality. This idea is mirrored in Kantian aesthetic theory when he says that the aesthetic experience hovers somewhere between actual perception and subsequent categorization.

We have now discovered all the necessary understanding of the structures of consciousness. We are ready to go back and relate this understanding to our description of art as it appears, which should enable us to understand why I said at the beginning that art could be considered the quintessential phenomena.

Which?

We have made our description, and we have analyzed the structures of consciousness, so now we can relate this to phenomena in its primary sense as that which shows itself. We said earlier that art is the quintessential phenomenon because its very being seems to involve showing itself. Now we can explain why this is so.

Art, because of certain characteristics which it has universally, tends to break the ready-to-hand structure of the world and engage the consciousness in a present-to-hand relation. Remember that we said that art lacks functionality in the usual sense. This lack of functionality creates an attitude of non-utility, which Heidegger calls obstinacy. This attitude of obstinacy prepares the way for the jump to the present-to-hand. However, this lack of functionality is not in itself sufficient to cause the breakdown in the world structure of the ready-to-hand,

The form of the work of art, and more specifically of artistic language, is organic. This organic form, which corresponds directly with the relation of the class as one, is not comprehensible within the mode of the ready-to-hand which as we said is based on the relation of the class as many. This tends to force the consciousness into the present-to-hand mode.

The content of the work of art is also responsible in part for the jump from the ready-to-hand to the present-to-hand. Specifically, the content of the work of art normally consists of certain tricks or devices that tend to break the rational perspective prevalent in the ready-to-hand mode of consciousness.

Consider the first quote we had from Keats' Ode on a Grecian Urn. Keats here uses the grammatical technique of ambiguous objects with the word still to ambiguate the whole line. In the second line quoted, Keats uses the paradoxical identification of beauty and truth to achieve the same effect. Both of these lines are rendered rationally income-prehensible by their content. In addition, on a deeper level, art seems to draw from those experiences which Langer terms the life of feeling. These experiences are similarly not formulatable in rational thought, and so contribute to the shift to the present-to-hand.

Lastly, we see that once in the present-to-hand mode we can account for the intensity and vitality of the experience of the work of art. The unmediatedness of the present-to-hand is certainly one source of this vitality. The fact that the present-to-hand relation is more primordial than the ready-to-hand is another source of this vitality.

In addition, there is a sense in which the consciousness, having entered into the present-to-hand relation with the work of art, is united metaphysically with the work, since all such relations create unities.

Wherefore?

Art is by its very nature a human creation that powerfully involves us in the most vital and profound of relations. In doing so, it enriches our experience and tells us about ourselves as human beings. In addition, just by our engagement in the present-to-hand, we become more aware and open to such relations within our whole environment, especially those ultimate relations with the universe, with our self, and with those we love. This is the value of art, and, I think, as fair and true a definition of art as can be made.

Who?

A Critique of Pure Reason, Immanuel Kant, translation Paul Guyer's & Allen Wood

Biographia Literaria, Samuel Taylor Coleridge,

Nature, Ralph Wadlo Emerson

Biographia Literaria, Samuel Taylor Coleridge,

Being and Time, Martin Heidegger, translation John Macquarrie and Edward S. Robinson

Sense and Nonsense, Maurice Merleau-Ponti, translation Herbert L. Dreyfus and Patricia Allen Dreyfus

Philosophy in a New Key, Suzanne K. Langer

Poetics, De Anima, Metaphysics, Aristotle

The Irrational Man, William Barrett

Problems of Art, Suzanne Langer

The Naked Ape, Desmond Morris

Philosophy of Art and Beauty, Hofstader and Kuhns, eds.

Art as Experience, John Dewey

I and Thou, Martin Buber

Art and Illusion, E. H. Gombrich

Aesthetics, Harold Osborne ,ed.

Laws of Form, G. Spencer Brown

ACKNOWLEDGEMENTS

*Why my Novel is Set in Minnea*polis was first published by The Rake magazine.

You May Quote Me was first published by Publishers Weekly.

What Would Shakespeare Do? was first published but Unbridled Books.

Where I Write was first published on The Next Best Book Blog.

How Not to Write a Sequel was first published in BlueInk Review.

Many of the other pieces have appeared on The Green Room at: https://www.gr8word.com

ABOUT THE AUTHOR

Stephen Evans is a playwright and the author of *The Island of Always, Whose Beauty is Past Change*, and *Funny Thing Is: A Guide to understanding Comedy*. Find him online at:

https://www.istephenevans.com/

STEPHEN EVANS

BOOKS BY STEPHEN EVANS

Fiction:

The Island of Always:

The Marriage of True Minds

Let Me Count the Ways

My Winter World

The Marriage Gift

Paradox

Whose Beauty is Past Change

The Mind of a Writer and other Fables

Epigrammaticon

The Next Joy and the Next

Non-Fiction:

Funny Thing Is: A Guide to Understanding Comedy

Prolegomena to Any Future Vacation

Layers of Life

Liebestraum

The Laughing String: Thoughts on Writing

Plays:

The Visitation Quartet:

The Ghost Writer

Monuments

Tourists

Spooky Action at a Distance

At the Still Point

Experience	*Three plays about Ralph Waldo Emerson*
Generations	*(with Morey Norkin and Michael Gilles)*
As You Like It	*(by William Shakespeare, adapted by Stephen Evans)*
The Glass Door	*(An adaptation of Hedda Gabler by Henrik Ibsen)*

Verse:

Limerosity

Limerositus

Sonets from the Chesapeke

The Crooked Mirror

www.ingramcontent.com/pod-product-compliance
Lightning Source LLC
Chambersburg PA
CBHW030858200726
48289CB00003B/806
* 9 7 8 1 9 5 3 7 2 5 6 3 9 *